This is a complete work! Pastor Toks, as some of us fondly call him, unveils herein the dual responsibilities of the Sovereign God *and* chosen man in the fulfilment of a predetermined purpose. Although Jacob was chosen by God, he still had to learn to make choices that would conform him to fit God's mould.

The book also reflects on how one can sustain and maximise God's Grace on the pathway to destiny.

The last chapter, *The Well of Jacob,* is a classic! It shows all leaders that significance is only attained through today's sacrifices, which eventually become a legacy for generations to come.

Read, enjoy and apply!

Pastor Sola Mene
Petra Ministries, Nigeria

In *The Destiny of Jacob,* Tokunbo Emmanuel unravels further truth from Bible narratives to wrap up *The Well-digger Trilogy.* As I gleaned, a line of truth donned on me. While it is true that "a predestined glory is subject to man's everyday choices," and that "a man must exercise his will to do God's will," one central truth prevails: *only the one enabled by Grace is able!*

Jacob, a born supplanter and master swindler, after an encounter with Grace, became the Israel of God. Grace showed up on both legs of his life journey, ensuring his destiny was not aborted. He was destined to win by the exercise of divine choice, yet it was Grace that did it all.

This easy-to-read book will illuminate your path and send you a fresh beam of hope like it did me. I encourage you to dig in right away!

Bode Akindele
The Incubator International, Canada

Having enjoyed the earlier books in the Well-Digger series, it is a privilege to write about this latest one. Once again, Tokunbo Emmanuel does not disappoint.

Here, the unfolding of Jacob's destiny is interwoven with many lessons for our own. Throughout the book there is a helpful balance between the calling and choosing of God, and the responding and outworking that rests with us. The positive confessions at the end of each chapter provide us with an effective means of applying the book's lessons in ways that will help us establish our own destinies.

The final chapter is indeed a highlight and stands as a testimony to Tokunbo's skill as a storyteller, as well as to his gifts as a Bible expositor. I could say more, but if I do, I would detract from your enjoyment of the narrative.

Read on and be drawn into the secrets of Jacob's legacy, even as you shape your own!

Thank you, Toks, on behalf of us all.

Dr. Hugh Osgood
Charis Communications, UK

In *The Destiny of Jacob*, God has used our brother, Pastor Tokunbo Emmanuel to expound great truths about the benevolence of God, the supremacy of His power and the wisdom in submitting to His guiding hand. All things truly work together for good!

I am grateful to God for the privilege of friendship and fellowship with this dear son of God. I recommend this book with prayers and gratitude to God Almighty.

Iyiola Tella PhD
The LightHOUSE, Yola, Nigeria

THE
DESTINY
OF
JACOB

Tokunbo Emmanuel

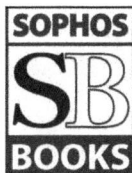

SOPHOS

SB

BOOKS

Raising the voice of Wisdom!

The Destiny of Jacob
Copyright © 2017 by Tokunbo Emmanuel

Published by
SOPHOS Books
163 Warbank Crescent
Croydon
United Kingdom
CR0 0AZ

ISBN 978-1-905669-85-1

Cover design by *Maestro Creativity*
Printed in the EU

CONTENTS

To Destiny, Daniel, David

& the generations after them.

AUTHOR'S PREFACE

Towards the end of 2005, I shared a message at my home-church in Bromley (UK), *Cornerstone Christian Centre*, titled *On Becoming a Well-digger*. A few months later, I published *The Secret of Abraham*. This small book, with its unique message and style, was the beginning of a new phase in my calling as a writer.

The Secret of Abraham was released and presented as the first of a trilogy. In my mind, I could see a book about Isaac and another about Jacob. However, I envisioned the end of these books, but not the journey towards this end. The next book to come to life in 2007 was not the book on Isaac, but another breakthrough writing titled, *The Greatest Well-digger In The World*. I found Grace to write *The Wells of Isaac* in 2012.

For a time, these three works were promoted as "The Well-digger Trilogy." Although I had the title of the book about Jacob in my spirit, I had no release to start writing, not even the chapter headings as is my custom.

The release came in this manner - O how grateful I am to God for these passage of events! At the turn of 2016, a dear pastor friend, Pastor Iyiola Tella, prevailed upon me to visit his congregation in Yola, the North-eastern part of Nigeria, as a speaker at a conference. When he asked me for a theme, what came to my spirit was *Stepping Into Destiny.* The accompanying Scripture text was Romans 8:28-30. A few months later, in August to be precise, I travelled to Yola for the meetings. We had such a powerful time with God and His Word during the conference, though I went with much fear and trembling.

Little did I know that God, through that weekend of ministry in Yola, was laying the framework for this book. For suddenly, two months after my Yola experience, I found the release to start writing *The Destiny of Jacob.* When I penned the chapter headings, it was evident to me that Yola, amongst other things, was a set-up by God for the conclusion of the well-digger trilogy (Pastor Tella had wished me to visit Yola many years before this visit, but this was the appointed time!).

I gratefully acknowledge, therefore, Pastor Tella and the entire *Lighthouse* congregation for the role they played in birthing this book. You are a testament to the Grace and power of God!

I also acknowledge some friends who lifted me up in prayer as I wrote this book. Thanks to Pastor Sola Mene, Pastor Dupe Obayori, Pastor Ben Adekugbe, Pastor Iyiola Tella and chief among them, Apostle Theresa Johnson, who also graciously wrote the foreword.

I want to specially acknowledge Dr. Hugh Osgood, a true father of the faith who has always been there for me and my family. Thanks, as well, to the church family at *Cornerstone Christian Centre*, the place we call home.

As always, I am grateful to God for my family: my dear wife Linda, and children, Destiny, Daniel and David. Your moral support is priceless.

Finally, I am eternally grateful to God who called me. From the onset, it was obvious that

He had a keen interest in this work. Without the strength and inspiration of His Spirit, I could not have seen it through.

Dear reader, the book you about to read drips with life. It is a fitting conclusion to the well-digger trilogy (and I hope you have read the preceding titles). If *The Secret of Abraham* reveals the *purpose* of well-digging, and *The Wells of Isaac*, the *process* of well-digging; then *The Destiny of Jacob* expounds on the *price* of well-digging. Anyone who would follow his God-ordained path and participate in God's divine agenda in the earth must embrace this three-fold commitment.

Now, may the well-digger message go forth and produce fruit that will abide for many generations!

- Tokunbo Emmanuel

FOREWORD

Tokunbo Emmanuel has been digging wells for as long as I have known him. God's Grace connected us across the nations through our passion for writing and his desire to learn more about being a prophetic scribe. I can still remember the testimony of how God took hold of his heart and pen, and held him lovingly captive until every single word He placed in him was poured out like incense on an altar.

While Tokunbo takes no credit for the unusual way our Father uses him to minister to His people, it is evident that he walks in ancient anointing – pulling revelation from the depths of the Spirit not only for himself, his family and those to whom he empowers in ministry, but also for this current and future generation of believers. Whether stepping into the fields of storytelling, prophesying the burden of a nation or speaking into the heart of a people, Tokunbo's longing to see others apprehend their destiny, move in purpose and walk in victory is evident. It literally seeps through all of his work. His books and blogs cry out for people to recognise, identify and embrace their inheritance in Christ, leaving a clear path for legacy to have its perfect work.

I assure you that these words are not my attempt to ingratiate an author; rather, I am identifying what I believe God has revealed concerning this aspect of his life. As sons of God, we are supposed to see the gifts and treasures in one another and honour them. In doing so, we surely honour God!

This latest work, *The Destiny of Jacob*, continues the burden God has given Tokunbo. By the time I reached the third chapter, I could hear Holy Spirit say: "We are all Jacob."

As you pick this book up for the first time, I want to challenge you to lay down any preconceived notions you may have concerning what "The Destiny of Jacob" is about. Jacob's life and testimony has been taught so many times that many of us might believe we can rehearse it in our sleep! I must tell you that even I have not heard Jacob's story told quite like this.

Expect to see and hear about yourself.

Expect to encounter God afresh and anew.

Expect to see the hard places in your life as opportunities.

Expect to appreciate and trust the journey that you are on right now.

Expect to encounter God's Grace at new proportions.

Expect to have a deeper understanding of why God CHOSE you!

This revelatory journey you are on will be well worth it.

By now, you probably know how much I respect Tokunbo Emmanuel. The apostolic grace upon his life is uncommon in this day and age. After all these years, meeting him and his lovely wife in person during his trip to Atlanta was clearly a part of God's plan. For me, it sealed what I have already known – our connection and relationship in the Lord was destined.

It is my prayer that those who read *The Destiny of Jacob* will come to know that God predestined them and that the only thing standing between them and their destiny is a choice.

Jeremiah 1:5a: *"I knew you before I formed you in your mother's womb."*

Theresa Harvard Johnson

The Scribal Conservatory Arts & Worship Centre

Voices of Christ Apostolic Prophetic School of the Scribe, Atlanta, USA

INTRODUCTION

Any discussion that centres around the destiny of a man would focus on the man but will, before long, move outside the remit of the man; for the essence of the word *destiny*, hovers in a realm where the divine meets the human. Inevitably, the superiority of the former over the latter will come to light in no small way. It also becomes clear that it is not given to man to direct his ways, yet man must yield completely to God for His ways to be divinely directed. Hence, this book is about God as it is about Jacob.

Jacob, the third of the Patriarchs, was a special character whose life abundantly consists of this unique interplay. His life journey reveals much about mortal man as it does about the immortal God. Here is a man who inherited a divine, generational covenant and was constrained to walk a unique path towards its fulfilment.

The significance of Jacob's journey is evident from the space Holy Spirit devotes to its detail. Unlike grandfather Abraham, whose beginnings in Ur were not recorded; and father Isaac, whose records are scanty at best, we have the privilege of knowing Jacob from the womb to his tomb.

In Jacob's story, we observe the dealings of God with man and man with God; we witness a rivalry between siblings that was of monumental proportions; we follow the twists and turns of a life full of pain and gain; we enter his love garden littered with roses and thorns; we encounter the strength of God undergirding the weakness of man.

As we consider Jacob's heritage and legacy, inevitably we find ourselves. More so, we find the triune God of Abraham, Isaac and Jacob.

Although Jacob was born into a lineage of well-diggers, and there is evidence that he dug wells in the land of his sojourn, the Bible does not focus so much on this land-possessing activity. There is more emphasis, it seems, on *who* Jacob *was* than on *what* Jacob *did*; on the *person* Jacob was *becoming* than the *land* he was *possessing*.

Jacob dug physical wells quite alright, but he needed God to first dig through the strongholds of his heart and release the virtues of life unto his seed and their seed. At the end, God accomplished this purpose in Jacob as much as Jacob, through God, accomplished his in the land.

This book, just like its predecessors, is a *concentrate* of wisdom and revelation. A good dose of meditation is required to fully distil its message and apply it to life. For the sake of maintaining a flow in reading, I have through-out used the masculine expression "man" but have in mind both men and women. Also, due to a revelation received in the process of writing, I have capitalised the word Grace, where I usually would have used lower caps.

Let us now, in this short treatise, explore Jacob's life and destiny, from the beginning before his beginning, to the end after his ending.

1

PREDESTINED IN ABRAHAM

(Genesis 12:3)

Long before God became the God of Jacob, He was first the God of Abraham, his grandfather. There would be no Jacob, as we know him today, without Abraham; and there would be no Abraham without God.

The essence of Jacob is contained in the person and calling of Abraham. Outside Abraham, Jacob has no lasting relevance. This simple and deep truth gives us a peek into the awesomeness of God and His eternal agenda. He knows all things before anything existed. He sees the end from the beginning. He sets the beginning before the beginning begins and in that beginning is an ending according to His good pleasure. He knew Jacob *in Abraham* and had great plans for his life.

The ability to know a thing before the thing is known is a characteristic that God alone possesses. He exists before time, in time and beyond time, all at the same time. From eternity's past to eternity's future, He is God. If any self-acclaimed deity can display even a tiny measure of ability to *foreknow* and *foretell* the future from the past, their claim to divinity could, perhaps, be worthy of note. This was God's challenge to all the gods that think they are God:

"Let them bring forth and show us what will happen;
Let them show the former things, what they were,
That we may consider them,
And know the latter end of them;

Or declare to us things to come. Show the things that
are to come hereafter, That we may know that you are
gods; Yes, do good or do evil,

That we may be dismayed and see it together.
Indeed you are nothing, And your work is nothing;
He who chooses you is an abomination."

(Isaiah 41:22-24)

Surely, it is an abomination to bow before wood or stone. It is foolish to commit one's destiny into the hands of things that are void of life. God alone is worthy of honour and trust. He alone knows "the latter end" of all things.

The thoughts that God have towards all men are only good. His plans are plans of peace and prosperity. No one is destined for failure or destruction; all are destined for a life of glory. It was so from the beginning, and in spite of the angelic rebellion, it is still so.

After sin was found in Lucifer and his subsequent expulsion from the heavens, God saw how far-reaching the effect of this contamination would be and sought to remedy the situation. If angels could fall, how much more man? So, ever before the first man was created; long before Abraham or his lineage existed, God set forth a redemption plan to restore all of creation. He required a spotless sacrifice to pay the eternal penalty of sin. This He provided for Himself in the offering of His Son; the giving of Himself. For the purpose of redeeming fallen man, the Lamb of God was slain from the foundations of the world (Revelation 13:8).

The cornerstone of God's redemption plan was the offering of His Son as a sacrifice for sin. This single act of love, set for a time to come, would forever deal with the power and effect of the adversary. Hence, when man did succumb to temptation in the garden of Eden, God spoke forth His predestined plan to redeem him: *"The Seed of the woman would crush the head of the serpent"* (Genesis 3:15). This "Seed of the woman," the epicentre of God's purpose, would, until a time appointed, abide in the womb of a nation that would abide in the womb of Jacob, who himself would abide in the womb of Isaac, who would abide in the womb of Abraham.

In other words, Jacob's destiny was intricately linked to the destiny of Abraham before him and the destiny of the Seed after him. The purpose of his existence was solely for the realisation of God's eternal plan of redemption - the plan to restore man and bless all of creation. Participation in this divine agenda is still the privilege of everyone God called since Jacob.

Jacob was predestined in Abraham and Abraham predestined in Christ. Through Abraham, and thus Jacob, all the families of the earth can come into this eternal predestination, this eternal blessing in Christ.

What did Jacob have to do to inherit the covenant blessing of God? Absolutely nothing, at least not of himself. His birth and election was enough to qualify him for the Blessing. Before he was brought forth from His mother's womb, God chose him. He was predestined in Abraham as a beneficiary of the covenant. Jacob did not earn this position; he was chosen. He was chosen to be the womb that would birth the pillars of the nation that would produce the Seed.

The truth and scope of God's foreknowledge is beyond man's comprehension. How can a finite mind comprehend or explain the actions of an infinite God? How does mortal man respond to this limitless dimension of the almighty God? There is only one response that is worthy of contemplation: *complete abandonment in life and worship.*

Why take life into your own hands when it is secure in the hands of God? Those who trust their entire lives (their past, present and future) to God like Abraham did, live to fulfil and enjoy their destiny. Severally, Jacob came to that place where he willingly entrusted his life's journey to the all-seeing, all-knowing, all-powerful God.

By responding positively to God's call and embracing, by faith, the promise of a brand new future, Abraham established the course of his unborn seed. He partnered with God's agenda to redeem man and bless the nations of the earth. His call was not about him or his need for a child, but about God's good pleasure and the plan to redeem God's creation. Through Abraham would come a people who would possess a *land* and produce the *Messiah*. The call was more than Abraham. It was also more than Jacob. The call was about Christ and His mission. Predestination, therefore, is a demonstration of God's love and redemptive intent.

It is worth repeating that God intended for man, created in His own image and likeness, to exercise divine rule over the earth and all created things. Walking closely with his Maker, man was meant to have dominion over the earth and produce a people after the likeness of God. But man, through an exercise of his will, chose the path of destruction.

However, long before man opened the door for sin to enter the world, God provided a remedy for its deadly effects - the Lamb of God slain from the foundations of the world. This divine sacrifice would restore man back to God and the earth back to man. All who believe in the Lamb and His sacrifice are baptised into Him, become partakers of Him and are destined to conform to His image.

Likewise, the Abrahamic covenant, a key component of the Lamb's emergence, which also preceded Jacob, set the course of the one who would inherit it. The beneficiary does not set the terms of the covenant, but having thus been called to inherit it, is conformed by it. Jacob inherited the blessing and the blessing conformed him accordingly.

The all-powerful God knows all things and holds all things together by His powerful word. This means His laws and principles are the very fabric of life here on earth. Positioning oneself against them only leads to destruction. A man who, knowing the laws of nature, *decides* to jump off a cliff in defiance, will face certain death. This is a kind of predestination.

In the same manner, the one who God calls into Christ must submit to the will of He who called him to be conformed to the image of Christ. Choosing to conform to another will inevitably hinder the realisation of a glorious destiny.

Jacob was called into Abraham's blessings and over his lifetime, he learnt to submit to the will of God who called him to a standard of living higher than the norm. In other words, although his predestination *preceded* him, it intimately *involved* and *shaped* him.

Today, we are grateful for and instructed by the lessons Jacob learnt throughout his life.

I am destined to win!

I am predestined for glory! God knew me long before my parents conceived me. He knew and called me in Christ. I am fearfully and wonderfully made for a divine purpose; to participate in God's eternal plan to redeem man and restore the earth.

God called me because He foreknew me, and I found Grace to say Yes to His call. How could I say No to a loving and gracious God, who has already blotted out my sins through the blood of His Son? Oh the joy of cleansing! The Grace for a new beginning! The beginning that He designed for me in Christ!

I now yield myself to the call of God, for unto the image of Christ I must be conformed.

I am blessed in Christ with all that is needful for life and godliness. I am a covenant child destined to impact my world for His sake. I in Him, He in me; success is sure!

2

THE BURDEN OF CHOICE

(Genesis 25:21-23)

There were two babies in Rebekah's womb, Esau and Jacob. One was needed to continue the Abrahamic covenant. It was not yet time for the twelve foundations of the nation, otherwise Isaac would have given birth to twelve; it was still the season for one - one that would take the third place in the triune arrangement. For there are three that bear witness throughout all ages and in all eternity. There must be three patriarchs by whom God would reveal Himself to the world. God chose Jacob, the younger of the two, to occupy this place, for there was only one place to fill. Only one could be chosen.

Again I say, for the plan of redemption and the mystery of trinity, God had to choose between Esau and Jacob. He had to choose one who would come into the covenant relationship. Out of the one would come the twelve. After the twelve would come the nation.

So, whilst the unborn children were being formed in the womb, God made His choice of both man and nation. In response to Rebekah's enquiry, God made His choice known and prophesied the destiny of the chosen seed:

> *"Two nations are in your womb,*
> *two peoples shall be separated from your body;*
> *One people shall be stronger than the other,*
> *And the older shall serve the younger."*

(Genesis 25:23)

The destiny of the one who would come after Isaac involved birthing the pillars of the Jewish nation. The Jewish nation was God's choice among nations, and Jacob was God's choice among two brothers. God foreknew him, predestined him and called him, even from the womb. He was preferred above his brother Esau.

Just as God created man with the ability to make choices, so does He also have the right to choose. In this instance, He chose Jacob and took upon Himself the responsibility for the choice He made (just as we are solely responsible for the choices we make in life).

Did God overlook Esau because he foreknew the kind of man he would become? Was it because his character was flawed? But Jacob also had imperfections in his person for they were both, through Adam, partakers of the sin nature. *God overlook Esau because He had to overlook one.* He exercised His right to choose, even if His foreknowledge aided His choice. If it was solely because of what Esau would be and do, then it was no longer by Grace. Eternal redemption is founded on Grace alone and not on works.

That God *chose* Jacob before he was formed does not mean that God *condemned* Esau before he was formed. God is not unjust. Man is condemned by his own choices and his choices alone. In Adam, man had already made a choice that brought upon him eternal condemnation. It is to reverse this order that He chose Abraham, Isaac and now Jacob. If man has a right to choose, God also has a right to choose.

Each one, both God and man, would bear the burden on his choice.

(Although God, through Malachi, said, "Jacob I *loved*, Esau I *hated*," we should understand this as a language of *preference* and not *abhorrence*. Needing to make a choice between the two, God *preferred* Jacob over Esau. This is akin to what Christ taught, that if circumstances require us to make a choice between God and earthly relationships, we should choose God and thus remain His follower. He taught us to prefer God over wife, children and earthly acquaintances; He did not instruct us to "hate" them in the manner we understand the word today—Luke 14:26).

Again, God chose one because He has reserved for Himself the right to choose. *"For He says to Moses, 'I will have mercy on whomever I will have mercy, and I will have compassion on whomever I will have compassion.' So then it is not of him who wills, nor of him who runs, but of God who shows mercy"* (Romans 9:15,16). God's choice, therefore, was by Grace because neither one of the two sons could qualify based on their deeds. God decided to show mercy to one, and the one was Jacob.

Every man born of a woman is imperfect in nature. Hence, from the onset, God knew that He would need to work *in* and *on* whomever He chooses to conform him to his destiny as a patriarch of Israel. This would be a work over a lifetime, one to which God was ready to commit.

This character-refining work within men chosen by God, a work to which God has committed Himself, also involves the will of men. As God works *on* men, they must also work *with* God. This highlights the importance of making right choices at every junction of life. For choices, whether good or bad, attract consequences, both good and bad. The choice Jacob made to deceive his father for the blessing of the firstborn (howbeit through the influence of his mother) had the inevitable consequence of the brother's fury attached to it.

Indeed, from the womb, Jacob had traits of one who would supplant another through cunningness and deception. It was ingrained in his character to make room for himself through crooked means at the expense of others. For this reason he was named Jacob. And for this reason God sent him to his uncle

Laban, a master deceiver, who would, in time, teach him not to deceive. Jacob would bear the burden of his choices and learn divine lessons along the path his choices charted for him.

Esau also had to live with the consequence of his choices. Pressured by his appetite, he chose a moment's satisfaction over the privilege of a lifetime. He threw away his birthright for a bowl of porridge. He gratified his flesh and devalued his spiritual heritage. One choice set the course of his life forever.

Every man's choice determines or alters the path towards his destiny. No matter how lofty the glory of his destination, by the exercise of his will in choosing, man can make *progress* or otherwise *regress*.

For Esau, it was not just what he chose to *do* under pressure, but also what he chose to *say*. With his own mouth he made nothing of his spiritual privilege and thus sealed his destiny. By saying, *"What is this birthright to me?"* Esau justified God's choice and confirmed that he was not worthy of the higher call (Genesis 25:32).

Job chose not to speak angrily against God and thus qualified himself for restoration and double blessings (Job 1:22; 2:10). With their mouths, the children of Israel brought death upon themselves and thus sealed their destiny in the wilderness. *"Just as you have spoken in my hearing,"* God told them, *"so I would do to you"* (Numbers 14:28). A forty-day journey lasted forty years because of a wrong *choice* and the wrong *voice*.

The wise among men would mind the choices they make *and* the words they speak under pressure, for these can largely affect their destiny. Words chart the course of a man either towards life or towards death.

Although God, from the beginning of time, can see the end of time, yet He is not a micro-controller of time. For in time and per time, man must exercise *his* will to do God's will. Predestined glory is subject to man's everyday choices - and God does not make man's choices for man. God did not create a pseudo-world of lifeless matter. He created man with a free-will and with his freedom to choose, man is a participator in his journey towards destiny.

God can work *in* man so that man wills to do what God pleases, but it is up to the man to make favourable choices and speak favourable words when it matters.

Every choice is borne out of a man's character, knowledge and sense of destiny. When character is skewed towards righteousness, knowledge rooted in the Holy and sense of destiny focused on unseen glory, then choices will favour both God and the covenant man. But when character is of the old nature, knowledge limited to the five senses and the awareness of destiny clouded by the lusts of this life, choices will consistently fall out of line with God's purpose. Two can only walk together when their core values are in agreement.

From whence came Jacob's appreciation of the covenant blessing? Is it not from his mother, who cherished within her the prophecy of his destiny? From whence came Esau's propensity to gratify the cravings of his appetite? Is it not from his father who loved him *"because he ate of his game"* (Genesis 25:28)? Herein lies an unbendable truth that impacts the destiny path of all men: *parental influence and daily interactions with their authority, especially in the early years, go a long way to set the course of a man's life.*

The words that a child continually hears spoken to him; the life that his parents model before him; the love or lack thereof by which he is nurtured; all these and more are factors that either make *straight* or *crooked* the path to a great destiny. Isaac's path, we can say, was smoothened because his father taught him with words and deeds. Perhaps we cannot say the same about Isaac and his sons. Why this was so, heaven alone knows.

Although parental choices of action place a burden of some sort upon their children, each man must take full responsibility for his own choices and habits. It is an exercise in futility to endlessly blame a troubled past when one, with intention, can begin to sow and nurture seeds for a great future today. You cannot reset the past, but you can redesign the future that your past has set for you. Jabez, in spite of a troubled past, reached out to God and the course of his destiny was altered forever (1 Chronicles 4:9,10).

Each man must carry his own burden, no matter how heavy. Are not all men bearing already the burden of Adam's fall? God's eternal plan to relieve man of this burden led to the call of Abraham and at each crucial junction, Abraham made choices that delighted God's heart. What could have befallen this grand plan if Abraham withheld Isaac on the mountain of Moriah? Abraham chose to offer him to God in faith and God responded with a promise that cannot be broken. All who are of the faith of Abraham are today partakers of this promise.

Jacob had to carry his own burden and learn to make the right choices. He would receive help from God, the burden-bearer, and submit himself to the destiny-shaping hands of God.

I am destined to win

What did I do for God to choose me? I am chosen by Grace; I am chosen in Christ. I choose to say Yes to the One who calls me by name. I exchange my heavy burden for the lightness of His life. I am now yoked with Christ and I choose to follow Him wherever He goes.

As God works in me and works with me, I surrender my will to His and choose conformity to the image of His Son. My choices in life are informed by His working within me. I see beyond the immediate and embrace the glory to come. When under pressure, I will find Grace to choose Him. Yea, not my will but His be done.

3

THE TWO ENDS OF GRACE
(Genesis 28:10-17)

I t is evident that God's way of dealing with man from the beginning of time is the way of Grace. Long before man chose sin, God provided a remedy. Before Jacob was fully formed in the womb, God called him to inherit a blessing. Before we were yet sinners, Christ died for the ungodly. We can safely conclude, therefore, that relating with mortal man on the basis of his works alone was not God's design. Our redemption is *founded on* and *fulfilled by* Grace alone.

Law is the opposite of Grace. Law says you are qualified because of what *you* do; Grace says you are qualified because of what *I* have done. Law says if you do and end well, your reward is glory; Grace says you are predestined for glory and for this reason, you will do and end well. Law requires man's righteousness before it can give access to God's fullness; Grace requires God's righteousness for man to access God's fullness. As far as the heavens are from the earth, so is the way of Grace far above the operations of Law.

Grace blesses super-abundantly even before the recipient of Grace has manifested a single work. Law, on the other hand, measures its blessings in accordance to the works of man. In truth, a single breaking of the law is enough to disqualify a person from its rewards. Who among the sons of men is able to fulfil such a stern requirement for blessedness?

God, knowing ahead of time that man would ultimately fall, provided the answer to man's failure *before* man encountered the question. All man has to do is choose God's answer and enjoy all His goodness. This is the way of faith. Attempting to provide an alternate remedy for or by oneself will always fall short of the mark of righteousness. God's answer is Grace, which says, *"I am always here for you."*

Again, God blessed Abraham not because of Abraham's deeds but because He chose to bless Him. All Abraham needed to do was say *Yes* to the One who called him and believe God without wavering (see Genesis 15:6; Romans 4:16-22). Isaac also inherited the Blessing. So did Jacob. All they had to do was believe the Blesser and their blessings were sure. (Evidently, Esau did not believe in the unseen privilege of being in covenant with the Unseen One, hence his choice to despise his birthright for a bowl of stew).

Oh that man would understand and fully appreciate Grace! Herein is the love of God revealed to the full. Jacob encountered this revelation in a most powerful way. His life and dealings with God portray the beautiful operations of this Grace.

One encounter turned Jacob's life around for good and filled him with much hope for the future. Of a truth, only one encounter with Grace is enough to establish the destiny of man. Grace met Jacob at his lowest point and raised him to the highest place - undeserved, unannounced and unsolicited.

Running from the consequence of his gross deception; removed from the bosom of his loving mother; facing the prospect of an uncertain future, Jacob was exhausted in body and mind. The day was drawing to a close, giving way to the darkness of night. Jacob had nothing, felt like nothing and was in the middle of nowhere. After a few yawns of exhaustion, he found a stone upon which he could rest his weary head. On this night, at this lowly place, Grace reached out to a dejected and needy man.

From a natural perspective, Jacob deserved his depressed state. The wages of deception are hardship and just punishment. But Grace gives a man what he does not deserve. Grace seeks out the unworthy and reveals the abounding love of God.

On this night of nights, Jacob had a revelation of the loving God of his fathers:

"Then he dreamed, and behold, a ladder was set up on the earth, and its top reached to heaven; and there the angels of God were ascending and descending on it.

And behold, the Lord stood above it and said: "I am the Lord God of Abraham your father and the God of Isaac; the land on which you lie I will give to you and your descendants. Also your descendants shall be as the dust of the earth; you shall spread abroad to the west and the east, to the north and the south; and in you and in your seed all the families of the earth shall be blessed. Behold, I am with you and will keep you wherever you go, and will bring you back to this land; for I will not leave you until I have done what I have spoken to you."

(Genesis 28:12-15)

What a picture of Grace! Between the lowliness of man and the loftiness of God, there is a gulf that a thousand good deeds cannot fill. At one end of Grace is fallen, sinful man; at the other is the exalted, righteous God. The eyes of God are too holy to behold sin and the face of man too shamed to behold God. Both God and man would forever remain apart if not for Grace - the Ladder that bridges the eternal gap between dust and divinity!

On this Ladder of Grace were angels ascending and descending. Jacob was no angel; he could not dare even a step. No, he was not saintly enough; he did not measure up. Yet, Grace reached down to earth and extended all the way to heaven. Grace lifted him from a place of rejection to a place of acceptance. Grace established purpose in Jacob's life and connected him to the covenant with Abraham and Isaac. Grace promised protection, provision and preservation. All Jacob could do was receive the blessings of this Amazing Grace through faith.

It is the goodness of God that leads men to repentance; not the judgements of God. An encounter with the goodness of Grace can transform a man forever. Whilst Law requires good works from man before giving its blessings, Grace gives its blessings, which causes man to respond with good works. The blessings of Grace also include the power to live right. Anyone who truly receives Grace will not only *want* to please God, but will find the power to do so.

Surprised and overwhelmed by the blessings of Grace, Jacob found strength to pray and make vows. He realised that he had a great purpose to live for and a great God committed to its fulfilment. He was, like his forefathers, destined to inherit a land and produce a people. When, through Grace, a man discovers that there is meaning and purpose to his life, a vision lays hold of his heart and places restraints on him throughout his journey. Oh that man would discover himself in God's Grace!

The place of this discovery is the foundation upon which significance and purpose is built. Jacob called this place Bethel, the house of God, for Grace is the place where the God of Abraham and Isaac resides.

Bethel was Jacob's place of discovery. It became the foundation of Grace that secured his destiny. What the mountain of Moriah was to Abraham, and Rehoboth was to Isaac, Bethel became for Jacob. Each one had his own encounter with Grace; each one had his own divine experience that sustained him on the path of destiny.

Grace is the beginning and ending of a glorious destiny. Grace says, *"I will not leave you until all my word is fulfilled in you."* This is Grace to the extreme! Grace is committed to your destiny!

A revelation of the commitment of Grace to a man's destiny causes man, in turn, to commit fully to Grace. Why leave the One who has promised never to leave you? Why offend the One who has already forgiven all your offences?

"I will not leave you" was a not just a promise of God's presence; it was also a commitment to conform Jacob to the image of covenant righteousness; a dedication to teach him divine lessons and work godly character within his person.

Grace *teaches* man to say "no" to ungodliness and worldly passions (see Titus 2:11, 12 NIV). Law *expects* man to say "no" - and there is a difference between the two. Grace is not a "yes" to every kind of device!

Over the course of his life, Jacob learnt lessons that only Grace can teach. The deception and shrewdness he endured from Laban were not punishment for his own deception and shrewdness; they were live lessons of Grace. After years of staying at home with his protective mother, he learnt the value of hard work on Laban's field. Twice he got what he wanted through cunning manipulation; for two seven-year periods he laboured and toiled for what his heart desired.

Surely, on the path of destiny that the choices and actions of man have charted, there are lessons of life that ultimately transform the life of the man. Every man's path is different. Every man's lessons will vary. At the end, Grace knows *how* and *what* to teach; Grace is able to bring the chosen man to the place of perfection.

Oh for a revelation of the operations of Grace! Only one encounter is enough to anchor a man to the love of God forever! From the time of his encounter, Jacob became conscious of God's unconditional presence. He understood deeply His calling in Abraham. He embraced the importance of possessing the land of promise and producing a people after God's heart. His awareness of the call deepened throughout the twenty years he spent in exile and beyond.

Even when it seemed like Jacob would leave his uncle a pauper, Grace came through for him and blessed him beyond his wildest imagination. *Oh for a revelation of the operations of Grace!*

I am destined to win

Oh for a fresh revelation of Grace in my life! All that I am; all that I ever would be is by Grace and Grace alone.

I am foreknown in Christ, by Grace.

I am predestined in Christ, by Grace.

I am called in Christ, by Grace.

I am justified in Christ, by Grace.

I am glorified in Christ, by Grace.

Grace is moulding me. Grace is teaching me. I submit to the dealings of Grace and embrace all the teachings through life. I am not what I used to be and I am becoming all He wants me to be.

O wonderful Grace and the angels thereof! I cherish this place of revelation. I forever commit to the God of my Bethel. I can never remain the same because Grace is still working in me.

4

MORE THAN A CONQUEROR
(Genesis 32:22-32)

Life is a journey. Life is a fight. The long journey of life is full of twists and turns. The intense fight abounds with struggles and battles. He who will fulfil destiny must learn to take the right steps at the right time and fight the good fight of faith. The greater the consciousness of God's calling by Grace, the greater the determination to endure to the end.

The calling of God is weighty but it does not crush the called. Everyone called of God increasingly understands that the destiny of many hinges on the destiny of one. Hence the need to always make favourable choices, especially in the face of conflict and pressure.

There will be countless "opportunities" to take the path of least resistance and give up the fight. But why forfeit a glorious destiny because of temporary comfort? Why truncate the destiny of future generations by quitting in the present?

Every encounter with Grace increases the consciousness that many lives depend on your life. God does not just bless a man; He blesses him and his seed. God blesses man so that man can be a channel of blessing to many. Those who would *walk* and *work* with God must prove themselves worthy of their calling by dying to self and living for the good of many. If man, by his selfish choices, foolishly positions himself not to receive God's generational favour, another would be sought to take his place.

Be sure of this: God will test the ones he calls. But He also gives Grace for the called to face the test and win. Grace begets grace. He does not subject us to tests for which He has not equipped us. Neither will He allow temptations that are more than our capacity to bear.

With every encounter Jacob had with God, his capacity to comprehend the mandate God placed upon him increased. The revelation of Grace at Bethel sustained him in the house of Laban. Though a fugitive in Padan Aram, he was assured of God's presence and God's promise. Deep down in his heart, and in spite of his prevailing circumstances, he knew that he was destined to inherit the covenant land and produce a covenant people. Thus he embraced two decades of labour without complaint, living by this philosophy of Job: *"All the days of my hard service I will wait, till my change comes"* (Job 14:14).

Two wives, two mistresses and eleven children down the line, it seemed as though Jacob's life will end in penury. He had a family but owned nothing else. He was miles away from the land of his calling and could not entertain the thought of returning. His night was long and his joy was still to come.

God makes all things beautiful in their proper time, especially for the one who learns to patiently wait for his due season. Jacob waited. And throughout his time of waiting, he did not swindle his uncle. Although he could justify himself for doing so, he chose not to. In essence, Jacob, passed his waiting test. He had learnt *how* and *why* not to dubiously make a way for himself. He had learnt to trust in God alone.

The lessons learnt during seasons of waiting are as important as the things we await. The person we are becoming on the path of destiny is as important as arriving at the port of destiny. We are destined for glory, yet we must *"glory in tribulation, knowing that tribulation produces perseverance; and perseverance, character; and character, hope"* - a hope that does not disappoint (Romans 5:3-5).

During the twenty years of Jacob's hard service, he could have found twenty justifiable reasons to steal from Laban. Instead, he lived clean. He even compensated Laban from his own sweat when wild animals or robbers depleted the livestock (see Genesis 31:38-41). But Jacob leaned entirely on the God of Bethel who justifies. He did not force his way, rather he remained in tune and in step with the Way-maker. He learnt to follow God's lead and not, in his own wisdom, take the lead.

And it came to pass! A fresh Grace encounter showed him the way and prospered him beyond his wildest imagination.

"And it happened, at the time when the flocks conceived, that I lifted my eyes and saw in a dream, and behold, the rams which leaped upon the flocks were streaked, speckled, and gray-spotted. Then the Angel of God spoke to me in a dream, saying, 'Jacob.' And I said, 'Here I am.' And He said, 'Lift your eyes now and see, all the rams which leap on the flocks are streaked, speckled, and gray-spotted; for I have seen all that Laban is doing to you. I am the God of Bethel, where you anointed the pillar and where you made a vow to Me. Now arise, get out of this land, and return to the land of your family.'"

(Genesis 31:10-13)

Jacob, by revelation, knew that his season of waiting was over. It was time to leave the "University of Hard Knocks" and make progress on his God-chosen path. Having built for another, He was now ready to build for his own. Yes, he was ready to build for God.

He who is committed to building for God would himself be built by God. He who sacrifices his life to seek God's interest would have his interests taken care of by God.

Heaven is not slow to bless in the manner in which man views slowness; but in the proper time, God makes all things beautiful. With one instruction, one idea, Jacob was blessed with the wealth of the wicked, much more than he could have acquired by trickery and deception. It pays to follow God. It pays to trust and obey.

Jacob prevailed over Laban but not in the way he prevailed over Esau. He conquered not by might or by power, but by the wisdom and revelation of God. He conquered by Grace! If he had employed the strength of cunningness, he would have lost the battle because Laban was a master at deception. But the upper limit of man's wisdom is no match for the least effort in Grace. One God-given idea will succeed far beyond a hundred conceived in the flesh.

With a camp full of covenant children, streaked-and-striped livestock and the presence of the Almighty, Jacob embarked on the tedious journey homeward. He obeyed God and set his face on returning to the land of his calling.

"So Jacob went on his way, and the angels of God met him. When Jacob saw them, he said, This is God's camp." And he called the name of that place Mahanaim."

(Genesis 32:1)

At this same place twenty years ago, Jacob, fleeing the consequences of his deception, had a revelation of Grace. Now, the angels of God were not ascending and descending the Ladder of Grace; they came to camp with him. These were ministers of Grace committed to bringing God's word to pass in his life. Surely, Jacob had come full cycle.

God's promise to Jacob never changed, yet, Jacob's past threatened to encroach on his future. With fear and trembling, Jacob braced himself to face the greatest battle of his life. It was time to face Esau and his four-hundred, battle-ready men!

The fiercest battles of life are fought alone. For a man is not what he is before men, but who he is in his solitary moments. The choices that really matter are made in this place of solitude, away from the glaring eyes of friends and foes. Such choices are influenced by core values of faith, an understanding of divine purpose and a sense of responsibility to the beneficiaries of destiny.

With great trepidation of heart, Jacob separated himself and sought to be alone with God. And in this place of aloneness, the battle for destiny raged.

Jacob, give up!

I will not. I cannot!

In the morrow, you shall meet your end.

Not with the great purpose over my life.

You do not deserve to live.

But God has preserved me for Himself.

You are a deceiver by nature.

But God has taught me His ways.

You must pay for your sins.

There is One who will pay for me.

The payment is a thousand deaths.

There is One who will die for me.

Why do you refuse to quit?

I am destined to win!

Jacob give up!

I will not. I cannot!

What would make a man to relentlessly hold unto faith when adverse circumstances pressure him to cast it aside in despair? What would make a covenant person keep his eyes on a distant reward when the present offers no consolation? Why did Jacob refuse to quit the fight when his body and mind were screaming for relief? How did he manage to persevere beyond his breaking point?

It was the same quality of determination and conviction that enabled his grandfather to raise his knife to offer his son, Isaac, to God on the mountain. It was the same faith that inspired Isaac to obey God and put precious seed into a parched land. God wanting to test Jacob's resolve to its limit, dislocated his hipbone and wrestled him to the point of near-submission.

However, Jacob just knew that God was *for* him and not *against* him; and if God was thus for him, no man or angel can stand against him.

Jacob realised that the weight of covenant glory that he carried within was the foundation for countless generations to come. Much more than his life was on the line; the promise and eternal purpose of God was at stake; the destiny of a whole nation hung on him. For the joy that was set before him, Jacob despised the pain of the moment. He concluded it was better for him to limp into his destiny than walk away in defeat.

Ignoring the excruciating pain in his side, Jacob tightened his grip on the one who wrestled him. He held unto God and refused to let go. Even when the angel sought to leave, Jacob clung on.

In a flash, Jacob recalled his past years and the Grace that had brought him this far. He concluded that in spite of all he possessed, only one thing mattered to his calling and destiny. With all the faith he could muster, Jacob asked for the Blessing of God - the abiding, undeniable, unstoppable, undefeatable presence of the God of his fathers, Abraham and Isaac.

The requests we make at crucial points in life reveal the divine working that has transpired within. Under much pressure and the temptation to preserve himself, Jacob did not ask for the death of his enemies. He did not ask for long life. He did not ask for silver and gold. He asked for the one thing that encompasses all things. He sought for the only thing that can guarantee his destiny. He asked for God Himself and He got what he desired.

In asking for the Blessing, Jacob sought to fortify not only his future, but also the future of his seed and their seed. If by virtue of the covenant Blessing he is destined to be a blessing to all the families of the earth, then Jacob's request was of great significance. In the most intense battle of his life, Jacob got the victory for his family, for your family, for all the families in the earth. For this reason, God changed his name.

He who would carry the weight of God's blessing must cross from death unto life. The old man with its old deeds cannot bear the fullness of God's glory. As Jacob acknowledged and surrendered his old self to God, he received a new identity that matched his destiny. No longer was he Jacob, the swindler; he was now Israel the prince of God! From this point on, he no longer bore the consciousness of his deficiencies; he was now, more than ever before, conscious of God's Grace and his destiny in God.

Jacob called the place of his transformation, Peniel, saying *"For I have seen God face to face, and my life is preserved."* And as he crossed Peniel, *"the sun rose over him, and he limped on his hip"* (Genesis 32:30,31).

Oh what a night! Oh what a sight!

Burdened through the thick of dark

Wrestling man or an angel arch

It's all or nothing; now or never

Past atoned; future secured forever

Oh what a night! Oh what a sight!

Slowed by a limp, upheld by a staff

The weight is lifted, there's peace at last

The rising sun ushers in a new day

Old Jacob is no more, Israel is born today!

The perseverance of one man is the deliverance of generations after him. The victory of one is the salvation of many. Reuben, Simeon, Levi, Judah, Isaachar, Zebulun, Dan, Napthali, Gad, Asher, Joseph, and the unborn Benjamin; these all were more than conquerors because of the transformation of Jacob. They did not witness the all-night warfare nor did they raise a fist in battle, but they are co-beneficiaries of the victor's crown!

As for Esau and his four-hundred-man troop, the line was drawn. How can you curse a man whom the Lord has blessed? How can you hurt a people whom the Lord protects? Fear cannot trouble a dead man. Death cannot harass a man who has passed from death unto life. Esau and his troop cannot attack a Jacob now turned Israel!

"When a man's ways please the Lord, He makes even his enemies to be at peace with him."

(Proverbs 16:7)

I am destined to win!

I cannot give up, I cannot quit. The One who called me is for me and not against me. Yea, He is interceding for me at the right hand of the Father.

I will see this fight through and secure a great breakthrough, not just for me but for the tribes coming after me. My darkest night will give way for a new dawn. My weeping will turn into great joy!

My mistakes of the past will hurt me no more. The guilt of yesterday is now swallowed up by Grace. My weakness has become my strength and all the mess in my life are material for my message.

In God I have found strength to overcome every adversary. Every tongue that judges me is silenced forever. I am an overcomer through Grace and my seed are more than conquerors. Yes, I have passed from death unto life!

5

THE WELL OF JACOB

(John 4:11,12)

W e have, thus far, gone back in time to discover the origins of Jacob's destiny - and indeed that of his fathers, Abraham and Isaac. We found that their paths were preordained from the beginning of the earth. These three Patriarchs formed the bedrock of God's redemption plan for mankind. Through their covenant walk, they were to inherit a land and produce a people from whom the Messiah would emerge to redeem the earth. Surely, through this blessed lineage, all the families of the earth would be blessed.

We noted that God, perhaps aided by foreknowledge, exercised His right to choose Jacob and not Esau. Having made His choice, God committed Himself by covenant to conform His chosen one to His image. Man also has the right to make choices and God does not interfere with man's exercise of the will. Yet, all choices have consequences, some more fatal than others. Man's choice to despise that which is spiritual and eternal in favour of that which is sensual and transient is most damaging. When such choices are sealed by unfavourable utterances, the effects are near irrevocable. Jacob prized the spiritual over the needs of his flesh. Esau despised the spiritual to gratify the cravings of the moment. God preferred the former over the latter.

Evidently, Jacob was chosen by Grace before he was formed in his mother's womb. God did not choose him because he was perfect. Yet, in choosing him, God committed Himself by covenant to raise Jacob unto perfection. The revelation of Grace at Bethel established the covenant of God's commitment to Jacob and Jacob's commitment to God. From that time onwards, Jacob learnt perfection through the things that he suffered at the hands of Laban and through the restrained choices he made on a daily basis.

Twenty years of toiling without compromising came to an end when, by Grace, Jacob acquired a great number of livestock from stingy Laban. On God's instruction, he took his large family and embarked on the journey back to the place of his calling. However, before stepping into his destiny, he had to confront the past that threatened to destroy his future. Alone, broken and fighting for life, Jacob refused to accept defeat. He held unto Grace when it was easier to succumb to condemnation. Through Grace he prevailed and God changed his name to Israel. Through this personal transformation, Jacob secured an everlasting victory for his seed and their seed. Israel, the nation, is more than a conqueror because of the tenacious faith of their limping patriarch! Till today, they *"do not eat the muscle that shrank, which is on the hip socket, because God touched the socket of Jacob's hip bone in the muscle that shrank"* (Genesis 32:32).

Not once have we, hitherto, made mention of the fundamental secret of Abraham, which is well-digging, operating in the life of Jacob. Through a commitment to digging wells all over Canaan, Abraham and his son Isaac possessed the land that God promised them by covenant. The wells they dug were statements and symbols of ownership of the land. The wells catered for their seed and their seeds seed, and through them, their influence spread over the land.

Did Jacob know this secret? Did he ever become a well-digger? Did he dig any well in the land promised by God?

Men are known by the fruit they bear, whether good or bad. The quality of fruit is revealed not in the moment but in time. In God's design, every fruit should have in it the seed of next generation's fruit. Next generation's fruit should contain seed for yet another. Thus the seed multiplies and the fruit abides. The first man in line must "fall to the ground and die." He must not live for himself. Surely, Jacob laid down his life before God, and God raised from him the pillars of His chosen nation.

Generational men are also known by the wells they dig, for those who live for self do not labour for the seed who will come after them. If, by chance, the self-driven engage in well-digging activity, the wells they produce do not endure; they cave in under pressure and in time cease to exist.

Well-diggers, as a matter of priority, raise their seed to become well-diggers. They labour for generations after them by imparting a generational vision into their seed. Thus their works abide. Even when adversaries maliciously seize and block the wells they dig, their well-raised seed will fight to reopen them and dig more wells of their own. Rehoboth, the well dug by Isaac, is a testimony of how generations possess the land and fulfil God's righteous purposes in the earth.

Again, did Jacob know the secret? Did he engage in the practice of well-digging?

The evidence of Jacob's well-digging exploits is not recorded in the book of beginnings. However, nearly eighteen hundred years later, the truth emerged that he was indeed a digger of wells.

"So [Jesus] came to a city of Samaria which is called Sychar, near the plot of ground that Jacob gave to his

son Joseph. Now Jacob's well was there. Jesus therefore,
being wearied from His journey, sat thus by the well.
It was about the sixth hour."

(John 4:5,6)

A well that faithfully serves communities after eighteen hundred years is no ordinary well! This well of Jacob is, surely, one of great significance. It establishes the eternal perspective of well-digging in the purposes of God. It underscores why anyone called to participate in the programme of God must become a digger of quality wells.

The Seed of Abraham, through whom all families of the earth would be blessed, "needed to go through Samaria" to visit this well. He did not visit Beersheba or Rehoboth. He chose to visit this unnamed well, the well dug by Jacob.

Again, the significance of this well and the Grace-encounter that occurred when Jesus visited it are undeniable. The testimony of the Samaritan woman that Jesus met there emphasised the natural importance of well-digging. Jacob did not dig this well for himself, but for the community that was developing around him. He also dug deep into the ground so that the well would endure for generations to come.

"The woman said to Him, 'Sir, You have nothing to draw with, and the well is deep... Are You greater than our father Jacob, who gave us the well, and drank from it himself, as well as his sons and his livestock?'"

(John 4:11,12)

Jacob's well endured many generations because it went deep into the earth.

Of greater significance is the spiritual *transaction* and *transition* that happened at Jacob's well. During this encounter with the Samaritan woman, Jesus spoke about living water flowing forth to everlasting life (John 4:13,14). This "living water" would flow forth from within Him, the Christ, and whoever drinks of it would also become a spring of everlasting blessing. Thus all the earth would be filled with the glory of God!

So, from this well, Jacob's well, Jesus declared the eternal purpose of God, howbeit in parables. He also demonstrated it by totally transforming the life the unnamed Samaritan woman. Two days after this woman's encounter with the Christ, an entire community of people was touched and saved by the Messiah because of her testimony!

Through well-digging, the patriarchs possessed the land and produced a people unto God. Through well-digging, their seed would possess the world and establish righteousness in the earth! Out of the bellies of the righteous would flow rivers of life-giving waters that would bless the earth!

It is not on record whether Jacob dug more than one well. However, the one he dug is sufficient in proving the essence of wells in God's agenda. The well he dug was deep and it withstood the test of time. This single well was, in truth, a representation of his life, for the dealings of God in his life were *deep* and *he* withstood the test of time.

After the encounter with God and Esau, another phase commenced in Jacob's life. God had not finished fashioning Jacob's life. There was a greater depth of maturity that God was going to accomplish within him. Indeed, the deeper the dealings of God in a man, the fuller his understanding of God's purposes and the greater the impact of his life. Deep would always call unto deep. Likewise, shallowness would always beget shallowness.

The wells that some dig are not deep enough to endure the forces of nature. The wells are not deep because the workings of God within them are not deep enough. The well of Jacob was deep because the dealings of God in his life were deep.

Surely, God accomplished a lot in Jacob in the two decades that he lived with Laban. But this was just the beginning. Not long after the encounter at Peniel, Jacob buried Rachel, the woman he loved, and would later live with the pain of 'losing' the son that he loved. Sandwiched between these two experiences, was the daily strain of bearing patiently with the development of his children. As God took time with him, he had no choice but to take time with them.

It is not given to man to know exactly how things will turn out in his life, but through faith he can know that all things shall be well. This inner knowing that God is at work, no matter what happens, is the mark of a man who deeply trusts in God and His promises. God does not bring a man so far only to abandon him. In all things, we works for the good of those who love Him and are called for a purpose.

Jacob grew in his love for God the more he experienced God's Grace. He knew God had called him for a divine purpose - to possess the land of Canaan and raise a great nation that would produce the Messiah of the world. Holding firmly unto these, even when circumstances were contradictory, kept him going until he saw the fulfilment of God's promises.

After many years of following God and trusting in His faithful, Jacob became so full of God. Out of the depth of his heart flowed prophetic grace to bless his children and his children's children. The blessed man became a blesser of men!

Jacob demonstrated fatherly authority and prophetic sharpness when he changed the name of his last son from Ben-Oni (*"son of my sorrow,"* named so by Rachel) to Benjamin (*"son of my right hand"*). He understood from personal experience the significance of names to a person's destiny; and having had his own name changed by God, Jacob refused to associate sorrow with one of the pillars of the coming nation (see Genesis 35:18).

Jacob also demonstrated a maturity of spirit far deeper than that of Isaac, his father. Isaac, as stated previously, loved Esau because he ate of his game, but Jacob loved Joseph for a deeper prophetic reason. (If it was just, as the Scriptures recorded, that Jacob loved Joseph because *"he was the son of his old age"* (Genesis 37:3), then Benjamin should have enjoyed this privilege. Both sons were born by Rachel, whom Jacob loved, and Benjamin, the last born, was the true son of his old age). As evidenced in Joseph's life, Jacob took time to teach Joseph about the God of his fathers and the purpose for which they existed as a people.

Furthermore, as Isaac's time of departure drew near, he needed to eat some venison before he could declare a blessing over his son. And once the blessing was spoken, he had little else left within him to bless his other son. (Nonetheless, Scriptures made mention of this as an act of faith by Isaac. Although *"His eyes were so dim that he could not see"* (Genesis 27:1), when he realised the blessing had gone to Jacob and not his beloved Esau, he declared, *"I have blessed him - and indeed he shall be blessed"* (Genesis 27:33). By faith, therefore, he left it all in God's hands). Not so Jacob! Out of the wellspring of a deep life, Jacob found the prophetic resource to bless all before him. Twice he blessed Pharaoh, the emperor of Egypt (Genesis 47:7,10). He also blessed his twelve sons, speaking prophetically into their future (Genesis 49).

Perhaps a fitting testimony of Jacob's deep well is the entry that was made about him in the great roll of faith.

"By faith Jacob, when he was dying,
blessed each of the sons of Joseph, and worshiped,
leaning on the top of his staff."

(Hebrews 11:21)

Jacob was able to bless not only his own sons, but his son's sons. He spoke accurately by the inspiration of the Spirit over Ephraim and Manasseh. He set Ephraim, the younger, over Manasseh, the older, demonstrating a sharpness of spirit and a weight of spiritual authority. Jacob's life *work* and *walk* with God became a solid stepping stone for generations after him.

Surely, this kind of spiritual depth is not just bestowed on men; it comes with a price. Jacob paid a price with a life given to the worship of God, by learning obedience through suffering and fully depending on the *staff of God's Grace*.

Ever since his encounter with God at Peniel, from which he limped into his destiny, Jacob's staff was no longer a mere rod for herding sheep; it became a symbol of his dependence on God's mercy. Times without number, Jacob had leaned on this aged staff, offering prayers to God for his children. Severally, he leaned upon the staff and thought about his "lost" son, Joseph. In the past, he had leaned upon the staff and wondered how his growing family would evolve into a great nation.

On this occasion, Jacob leaned on his faithful staff, looked back over his life's journey and worshipped God for His faithfulness in bringing him thus far. From this place he also looked ahead and was confident of God's continuous faithfulness. Everything that God promised him by covenant, He performed, and would yet perform to the letter.

Although Jacob's God-given vision tarried, it spoke clearly in the end. The vision restrained, conformed and dug deep into him until he became a "well" capable of blessing countless generations after him. Surely, *"the end of a thing is better than its beginning."* He who follows God and endures to the very end will have the same testimony about his destiny; that *"He who calls... is faithful, who will also do it"* (1 Thessalonians 5:24).

Jacob breathed his last in Egypt, but, according to his wish, his body was buried in Canaan, alongside Abraham and Isaac. He was honoured with a grand ceremony that caught the attention of the neighbouring peoples.

From the womb to the grave; from his predestination to its consummation, Jacob experienced the faithfulness of God through and through. The people he left behind did become a great nation, and four hundred years later, they also returned to the promised land with a great deliverance and great wealth. Thus God's word to the founding patriarchs came to pass. Not a word fell to the ground unfulfilled.

I am destined to win!

God is accomplishing a great work within me and through him I am able to work without. My works shall endure the test of time and the test of fire. I will struggle no more even when I do not fully understand all that He is seeking to accomplish with me.

Of this I am persuaded, that all things are working together for my good. Yea, out of the depth of His dealings in me shall flow rivers of Grace that would bless generations to come.

I will follow through to the end. I will shun the frivolous for that which endures. I will produce a tribe after my own kind, after His image accomplished in me.

I will fight the good fight.

I will stay the course.

I will finish my race.

I will, in the end, receive a crown of glory. I will hear Him say, "Well done, good and faithful servant. Enter into the joy of your Lord."

POSTSCRIPT: I will arrive!

(An adaptation of Romans 8:28-39)

That place called destiny, I will arrive, for I know that all things are working together for my good. God is working in and for me because He has shed His love abroad within me and has called me according to His purpose. He foreknew me and predestined me to conform to the image of His Son, in whom I find Grace and through whom I learn daily to make the right choices that honour Him. I am now one of many brethren, Christ being the first.

Moreover, God called me, justified me and has glorified me. He completed His work in me and is leading me towards this completion. Surely, I will arrive.

What shall I say to these things? If God is for me, who can be against me? If He is so committed to my destiny, who can persuade Him to work against me? He who did not spare His own Son, but delivered Him up for me, how shall he not with Him also give me all things? Who shall bring a charge against me when I stumble and fall? It is God who justifies. Who is he who condemns? None can, for

Christ died, and furthermore is risen, and is now at the right hand of God making intercession for me. Who shall separate me from the love of Christ or stand in the way of my destiny? Shall tribulation, or distress, or persecution, or famine, or nakedness, or peril, or sword?

Yes, according to the written word, I may face hardship and death along the way; and people may consider me as sheep for the slaughter just because I am following the path God has charted for me. Yet, in all these things I am more than a conqueror through Him who loves me! Yes, I will arrive!

I am fully persuaded that neither death nor life, nor angels nor principalities nor powers, nor things present nor things to come, nor height nor depth, nor any other created thing, shall be able to hinder my destiny or separate me from the love of God which is in Christ Jesus our Lord.

By Grace alone, I will arrive!

Join the Well-digger community!

Www.facebook.com/WellDiggerCommunity

GET ALL THE

WELL-DIGGER BOOKS!

The Secret of Abraham

The Wells of Isaac

The Destiny of Jacob

The Greatest Well-Digger in the World

*"I am delighted that Tokunbo Emmanuel has
developed this thought-provoking series."*

- Dr. Hugh Osgood

Other books by
Tokunbo Emmanuel

The Shift of A Lifetime

The Mandate of Paul

Faith Clinic Revival

Run, Church Run!

Ultimate Destiny

The Charismatic Agenda

A Scribe's Inspiration

Rediscovering God

Revival in the Desert

Selah Verses

Sharing the Word of God

The Glory of Young Men

31 Nuggets of Inspiration